DROP SHIPPING BUSINESS

2023

A Comprehensive Guide

Sam Skinner

Table of Contents

Chapter One

One well-known way to generate money online is via dropshipping. Its easy setup is mostly responsible for its appeal.

This post will outline seven stages for getting started with dropshipping and some of the industry's best practices. We'll also go over the advantages of beginning a dropshipping company and the business strategy itself.

The advantages and disadvantages of beginning a dropshipping company by building your own website vs utilizing an eCommerce marketplace will also be contrasted in this lesson.

We will address some commonly asked questions concerning dropshipping at the conclusion of this post.

7 Steps to Launch a Dropshipping Company

1. Choose a niche for dropshipping

2. Do a market analysis

3. Locate a drop-shipping vendor

4. Establish Your Internet Shop

5. Compile the financials for the dropshipping business.

6. Create a legal structure for your drop-shipping business.

7. Improve and Promote Your Dropshipping Company

Why Start a Dropshipping Company?

- Platforms that Work Best for Your Dropshipping Company
- Establish a Website
- Establish a Store in an eCommerce Directory
- How to Start Dropshipping FAQ: What to Avoid When Starting a Business
- Is it Simple to Start Dropshipping?
- Does Dropshipping Pay Off?

- Can Dropshipping Be Profitable?
- Is it Possible to Launch a Dropshipping Company for Free?

Why Would You Dropship?
Dropshipping is a form of order fulfillment used to sell goods online from independent vendors. Businesses often choose this approach to avoid managing inventories and logistics. Instead, dropshipping businesses place a strong emphasis on marketing and branding their products.

Dropshippers establish business relationships with chosen suppliers and manage all fees and communications. A third-party manufacturer, distributor, or retailer might be the provider.

These are a few well-liked forms of dropshipping:

Reseller. For their online businesses, dropshippers hunt for merchandise from various vendors. The most frequent kind of dropshipping company is product reselling.

business growth. To sell its items online, a dropshipping firm might also collaborate with other merchants.

customized goods. Customers have the option to customize the product when using this type of dropshipping. Depending on the collaboration, dropshippers may also advertise goods under their own brand and label. As a result, many clients cannot tell a dropshipping company from a typical internet retailer.

What Is the Process of Dropshipping?
An illustration of the dropshipping model's first three phases

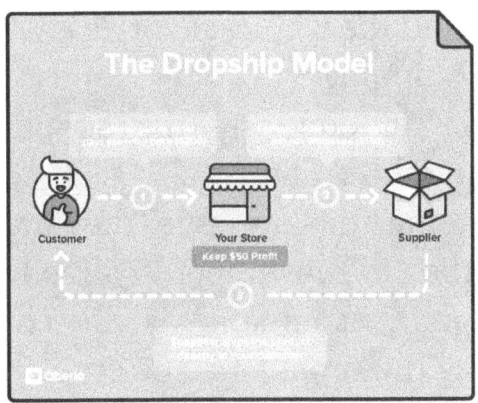

The buyer, the dropshipper, and the supplier are the three main participants in the dropshipping business model. The general method is as follows:

A consumer will pay the retail price for a product from a dropshipper when they make an online purchase.
The supplier will get the order from the dropshipper. Based on the terms of the

contract, the dropshipper gives the supplier the wholesale price while keeping the profit margin. For instance, the dropshipper will retain the $30 if the buyer pays $100 for a product and the wholesale price is $70.

Direct shipping of the goods to the consumer is done by the supplier after processing the order.

If a customer has an issue, they may speak with the dropshipper directly. The dropshipping company is in charge of informing the supplier of the problem.

7 Steps to Launch a Dropshipping Company
These are the first seven stages to starting a successful dropshipping company:

Select a specialty. Make a business plan that focuses on the merchandise you wish to sell. Analyze the market. Do a market niche analysis. Next, to make wise business selections, examine your competition and target market.

Locate a drop-shipping vendor. Choose reputable vendors that will provide goods that accurately reflect your own brand.

Organize an internet shop. Create a dropshipping website to sell items and develop your brand.

organize your money. Keep your personal and company accounts separate so you may track your dropshipping earnings correctly. Moreover, confirm if your dropshipping company must charge consumers sales tax.

Register your company as a legal entity. Before registering your dropshipping company shop, do some local law research. Keep in mind that every place has its own set of laws.

Improve and promote your brand. Use several eCommerce platforms and marketing tools to optimize your online business and advertise the items.

Starting a dropshipping company won't take much time or money if you do the necessary research and planning.

1. Choose a niche for dropshipping

Gather your dropshipping business ideas first, then identify a market niche for your company. This will make you stand out from other companies and discover acceptable providers.

A collection of goods that appeal to a certain market with shared interests is known as a dropshipping niche. The size of your niche will depend on the nature of your firm.

For instance, Meowingtons is a dropshipping business that offers goods to people who own cats.

Meowingtons's website

Create a dropshipping business plan first by deciding on the items, target markets, and objectives. This will aid in directing your choices in the subsequent phases.

Here are some suggestions on selecting a niche to build a successful internet business:

Decide what you are passionate about. Managing a dropshipping shop is more pleasurable when you are enthusiastic about what you offer. Also, selling your stuff to clients will be simpler.

Develop a resolution. Consumers choose dropshipping companies that provide answers to their issues. Get the proper items for your target audience by learning what they desire.

Put longevity first. To locate things that consumers will constantly need in the long run, use a free tool like Google Trends. Household appliances are one kind of commodity that never goes out of style.

Don't be scared to use creativity when you launch a dropshipping company to differentiate yourself from rivals.

Prepare a market analysis 2.

After you have a niche-specific dropshipping business strategy, do market research to evaluate the sector you are entering. The primary rivals and target markets should get the majority of attention in the market study.

Before starting the dropshipping business, it is crucial to do market research since you may quickly switch to another specialty if the findings are unimpressive.

To get your market research going, look at the following components:

Market size and industry value. Find out the size, trends, and growth rate of your market niche. This information reveals the amount of potential clients for the items. This approach may be assisted by tools like Semrush.

target market. Think about the age range, gender, economic level, interests, and profession of your target population. The profitability of your dropshipping company concept will be determined by this information.

Consumer purchasing patterns. To determine what influences product demand, study customer behavior. It will also be helpful to know how often customers buy comparable goods to set selling pricing.

principal rivals. Locate rival websites and evaluate their results. Similar web is only one of numerous internet resources that may be used to find market inefficiencies. Focus your study on five or fewer rivals, and consider their advantages and disadvantages.

You may use this research to create predictions and well-informed choices for your dropshipping company. It will be simpler to develop marketing strategy and estimate earnings.

Chapter two

3. Locate a drop-shipping vendor
Choose dropshipping providers if the market study shows promising outcomes.

Your dropshipping business's success may depend on your ability to find dependable suppliers. Suppliers are in charge of not only supplying the goods but also getting them to the consumers.

A broad selection of items are available from well-known wholesale vendors including Doba, SaleHoo, and Wholesale2B. A few dropshipping vendors, like Printful, can make unique items for your clients.

Take into account the following factors while looking for a supplier:

repute and legality. Look for a vendor with a good standing. To prevent con artists, always look at the supplier's customer list and request their company license.

online standing. To evaluate the service quality of the provider, look for independent evaluations.

Pricing. While selecting vendors, take the affiliate fee into account. Most dropshippers strive for profit margins of 15% to 20%.

Consumer support. Call the provider directly to see whether they offer helpful and kind customer care.

product excellence. Prior to reviewing the items, place your order. The majority of vendors let you try out their goods for free. Keep in mind that the provider should produce goods that reflect your branding.

shipping and packaging. Check to see how the goods appear when it is delivered and if the provider uses uniform packing and delivery methods.

procedure for completing orders. Take note of how long it takes the provider to complete and deliver the order. Choose a provider that can effectively manage returns as well.

Minimum purchase. Check to see whether the provider has a minimum order that requires upfront payment. Having this knowledge will help you set your price.

Integration. The majority of vendors provide connections to well-known e-commerce sites like Shopify, eBay, and Amazon. By selecting vendors that interface with these systems, you may streamline your dropshipping operation.

Analyze comparable items. To evaluate the quality and service of several providers, order comparable goods from each one. Choose the one that best reflects your dropshipping company.

To prevent discrepancies, we advise small businesses to only use one supplier. As your dropshipping company expands, think about using many suppliers to increase the range of products you can provide.

4. Establish Your Internet Shop
It's time to start your own internet shop now that you have goods to offer.

Then, decide on a name for your store's company. It should be distinctive, simple to remember, and ideally connected to your target market.

Choose a platform next for your dropshipping company. We'll contrast the two common ways to launch an online store: building a website and using an eCommerce platform.

Next, make sure your online business has consistent branding. The shop should have consistent branding to stand out from rivals even while the items are from outside vendors.

Warmly is a great illustration of how a dropshipping company can have an opulent design and powerful branding.

warmly welcome
To build a successful dropshipping business, pay attention to the following:

user encounter. Consumers have to be able to easily navigate your online store and discover the things they're looking for. Be sure to keep the user experience in mind while creating your website.
the payment gateways. Several payment choices and instructions should be provided. Be open and honest about any taxes and shipping expenses that clients must take into account.
Categories. Create distinct categories to make it simpler for shoppers to discover

your stuff. For quicker access, be sure to add the categories to your main menu.

merchandise pages. Provide thorough and detailed explanations as well as top-notch product images.

Message form. Offer prospective buyers a convenient way to inquire about your company and goods.

optimized for mobile. Make sure your business is responsive to mobile devices. Products should be available for purchase on many screen sizes.

Chapter three

5. Compile the financials for the dropshipping business.
Before you begin selling things, it is crucial to have your money in order.

Noting earnings and spending is simpler when your personal and corporate funds are kept separate. Also, doing so will benefit your legal procedures.

While setting up the financing for your dropshipping company, take into account the following:

bank account for a business. Create a brand-new company bank account in your dropshipping name. Keep in mind that you should only do business using this account, such as paying suppliers and receiving money from clients.

certificate for resale. In many places, selling goods purchased elsewhere requires firms to get resale certifications. If you need to register and pay for this certificate, check with your city or state.

income tax. In several nations, consumers must pay sales tax. Consult the local government of your company and its suppliers on the rules governing sales tax nexus. Then, be sure to include this expense in the price of your items.

Fee for maintenance. In order to sustain and expand your company, including platform fees and marketing expenses into your pricing and planning.

6. Create a legal structure for your drop-shipping business.

Important! In no way does Hostinger provide legal counsel. Just a broad overview of the legal considerations is given in this section. Before selecting your company's organizational form, we advise talking with appropriate legal bodies.

Organizing the legal aspects of your internet company is a further crucial step. This includes determining if dropshipping is legal where you are. Always do your homework for your nation since various places have different laws.

To submit taxes and apply for wholesale dropshipping accounts for companies in the United States, you will need a sales tax ID and an employment identification number.

Consider creating a lawful company after researching the laws to shield yourself from responsibility. Also, doing so could help you find more beneficial business partners and suppliers.

The three most typical business formats are as follows:

single-person business. Your dropshipping company funds will be subject to personal income tax under this arrangement. This is a dangerous choice since your personal assets are legally linked to your corporation.

Limited-risk enterprise (LLC). Due to the fact that your company will be treated as a distinct legal entity thanks to this structure, your personal assets will be protected. But, as a company owner, you must adhere to several regulatory criteria while paying taxes.

Corporation. This choice registers the dropshipping company as a distinct legal entity, much like an LLC. Instead of a small group of company owners, companies are controlled by directors and owned by shareholders.

We advise drafting the following records after registering the firm structure to win over clients:

Refund procedures. A clear refund policy encourages client loyalty since it shows that your dropshipping company is a safe location to make purchases.

Policy for returns or exchanges. Since they can't instantly view the goods, most buyers are reluctant to make purchases from internet merchants. A return or exchange policy increases consumer trust in your goods.

Conditions and terms. By having a legal agreement describing your company's and customers' rights and duties, you can manage expectations and safeguard your business.

Privacy statement. Describe the processes your company employs to gather, utilize, and disclose consumer information. This paper demonstrates how seriously your company takes its obligations.

Chapter four

7. Improve and Promote Your Dropshipping Company

It's time to market and sell your goods once you've established a legitimate drop shipping firm. For a dropshipping company to be successful, it is important to have effective marketing and client acquisition techniques.

Start with the following low-investment marketing techniques if you run a small business:

optimization for search engines (SEO). To increase traffic, every online company strives to rank better on search engine results pages (SERPs). The SEO of your shop may be improved to draw in more prospective clients.

Blog. In order to educate people about your dropshipping items, provide informative and consistent content. Moreover, connecting with audiences via blogging might benefit your company.

Email promotion. Create an email list by including a subscription form in your shop and rewarding new subscribers with a special offer. Moreover, email marketing helps retain current customers enthusiastic about your items.

the internet. Use various social media sites to share your content and goods to reach a wider audience. This marketing strategy also aids in maintaining consumer relationships for your company.

As an example, Notebook Therapy demonstrates how to use social media to increase reputation and engage with customers.

Facebook page for Notebook Therapy
As your dropshipping company expands and you have a larger budget, take into account the following marketing tactics:

Ads. The use of paid advertising to target a certain demographic is highly recommended. The majority of companies include Google AdWords and Facebook Advertising in their marketing plans.

marketing using influencers. Work together with well-known, influential individuals in the field. You may expand the audience you reach and strengthen the reputation of your company by having influencers promote your items on their channels.

affiliate promotion. Each time a consumer uses an affiliate link to purchase your goods, pay the affiliate a commission. This marketing tactic is a low-risk and economical approach to advertise your company.

Why Start a Dropshipping Company?

Due to the fact that you won't need to handle inventory and logistics, the dropshipping business model is a perfect method to launch your own online shop.

Dropshipping is often appropriate for small company owners, but bigger organizations looking to expand may also benefit from this approach.

These are some of the primary advantages of launching your own dropshipping company in case you are still on the fence:

minimal initial expenditures. You can operate a dropshipping company without keeping inventory on hand. You don't need to spend a lot of money up front to start selling things.

business plan with less risk. Dropshippers may quickly replace underperforming items from suppliers with new ones.

low levels of supply chain management. Offer your goods without having to manage logistics for shipment and stock up on inventory.

Adaptable place. Because you don't need to handle the items in person, you may operate and manage your company from any location with an internet connection. Dropshippers must, however, stay in touch with their clients and vendors.

many product choices. You may offer more things in your business since you don't need to have inventory on hand to make a transaction. You may change to a new product if the one you are using isn't working well.

a great deal of scalability. You can quickly enter a new market. You don't need to be concerned about getting additional orders since suppliers handle shipment.

But, running your own dropshipping company has significant disadvantages.

sudden shortages of supply. Suppliers may not always let you know when a product is running low in supply. To avoid advertising unavailable items in your shop, it's crucial to often check in with your suppliers.

lower level of control. In order to develop, package, and distribute high-quality items, dropshippers primarily depend on suppliers. You won't be able to immediately address problems like improper product handling, poor packing, or delayed delivery. Having said that, the benefits of the dropshipping model still outweigh the drawbacks.

Platforms that Work Best for Your Dropshipping Company
The majority of the labor is put into building a top-notch business since dropshippers do not have to worry about controlling product suppliers. The location of your sales has a big impact on the success of your dropshipping company.

Your platform has an impact on both how well your online business performs in terms of sales and how people see it. Starting your own eCommerce site and selling on a recognized eCommerce marketplace are the two most common platform choices for a dropshipping company.

We will discuss the advantages and disadvantages of the two solutions in the sections that follow. Keep in mind that you have the option of using several platforms for your shop.

Establish a Website

Having your own eCommerce website gives you greater control over the look, feel, and user experience of your shop.

Thankfully, if you choose the correct platform, you can create a website in less than an hour.

High-quality templates with a drag-and-drop editor are often available from website builders for your shop. For instance, the Hostinger Website Builder has tools like shipping interfaces, payment systems, and contact forms that are essential for a business.

Using a content management system (CMS) to build a website is an additional choice. WordPress, PrestaShop, and Shopify are a few of the well-known CMSs for e-commerce.

Install WooCommerce on your website using WordPress to add eCommerce capabilities. PrestaShop and Shopify, however, already have eCommerce functionalities built in. An easy 1-click script installation is included with Hostinger's WordPress hosting plan, which is an alternative.

The following are the main advantages of creating a website for your dropshipping business:

increased branding. You will have complete creative control over your branding with a website, from altering the theme to adding practical functions.

outstanding flexibility and control. Choose the information to include and the presentation style for your items. You may also choose the shipping and payment options that work best for your company plan.

higher margins of profit. Expect to get 100% of the proceeds from your sales as you are not paying a marketplace any platform fees.

no direct rivalry. Potential clients are the only visitors to your online store. They won't be able to view items from your rivals when exploring your website.

But, creating your own website has drawbacks as well:

higher start-up expenses. To build your own website, you'll need to pay for web hosting and a domain name. Several online markets, however, allow you to start selling for nothing.

There is no certainty of traffic and a mature market. Using eCommerce marketplaces, you may draw in a sizable consumer base for your shop. With a personal website, however, you will have to generate the traffic yourself.

How to Build a Successful Online Shop

You need a mechanism for customers to buy your products or services in order to do business online. But, you should consider the information you offer to your prospective clients — and how you express it — rather than simply the technical aspects of constructing a website.

Once you have a foundational website, converting it to an e-commerce business is a simple process. However this phase needn't consume a lot of time or effort. The process of creating content begins here. What about marketing, though?

The responsibilities in front of you might easily blend together, but this approach will help you compartmentalize them and create content that distinguishes you from your rivals.

Divide the tasks into three categories to assist yourself:

1 Install a shop automatically. You may simply host items and handle transactions on your existing website using add-on software.

2 Have an ethos and attitude that inspires trust in even strangers who do business with you. Create a tale that holds their attention from beginning to end.

3 Learn how your website fits with the larger Internet to spread the word about it (among your competitors and allies).

Let's examine how these three elements combine to create a successful e-commerce website for you.

1. Install an Out-of-the-Box Shop
Fortunately, you can easily add an e-commerce shop like WooCommerce once you have a simple website on a platform like WordPress.

Since the components are already built for you, implementation is fast and simple. Creating your product listings may take some time, but keep in mind that they fall under the category of "content," therefore it's helpful to divide these three sections.

Pick a platform like WooCommerce or Shopify so that you can effortlessly integrate their out-of-the-box software into your website. Now, you are able to safely complete transactions with only a few clicks.

See our blog, which outlines the many methods you may handle transactions on your website, for additional specifics on adding payment options.

2 Develop a personality and ethos
What matters most is this, and here is where you can truly start to shine. The section that demands a lot more of your time and attention. It's the element that makes up your brand specifically, making it essential to its success. That has to do with your online persona.

Consider your content to be the "narrative" that site visitors, no matter who they are, can connect with and be persuaded by. If you're starting from scratch, writing your narrative will need creativity, exploration, and possibly a lot of editing to get it just right.

But, if you are creating this website to complement an existing audience (for instance, a social media group), you may already have a tone of voice. Try to identify the key elements that have contributed to its success so far.

Create a Powerful Landing Page

Don't let the onslaught of information that follows scare you away! The most difficult page to get properly is your homepage since it serves as an overview of your whole website and attempts to tell prospective buyers all they need to know without them having to go anywhere else.

Before you get started, you may want to sketch out your ideal customer journey. This is the path that a client would travel if you left them a trail of breadcrumbs in an ideal world. This will be useful when you analyze

Google Analytics data on consumer behavior.

There are numerous parts you may include, from testimonials to how-to manuals, but the following components are essential for all homepages.

Headline and catchphrase:
The headline should simply and directly mention the name of your website. It is preferable for you to get your site to connect to the kind of company it is: "Lumos Luxury Candles" if you haven't yet given it a name. This will make your website easier for Google and other search engines to comprehend and will make it extremely apparent to anybody who sees it in a search result what it is.

Inventing Your Own Names

The naming procedure is really complex. Since it's challenging, many hire naming consultants to assist them.

To have a better understanding of the kinds of names that corporations are selecting, you might pose as a naming consultant. This will assist you in making the appropriate domain investments.

I name things, is how Anthony Shore, of the naming agency Operative Words, likes to sum up what he does.

It seems easy enough, but as Altman taught us, there is a lot that goes into naming things.

On a podcast, Shore discussed some of the methods he used. The same tools may be used by you to start your own namer business.

Here are five resources to look into:

OneLook.com - This resource contains thesaurus and wildcarding features. A namer's closest buddy may very well be a thesaurus. After deciding on a subject, seek for terms that have a similar meaning and might work well as brand names.

Sketch Engine: This is a powerful yet a little challenging tool. You may obtain a free trial and it is reasonably priced.

Discover rhyming words, synonyms, adjectives, and other terms with RhymeZone.

MRC Psycholinguistic Database - Useful for wildcards, replacements, etc.
A well-known dictionary search tool that lets you search numerous dictionaries is called GoldenDict.

The Domain Is Not Always Important
You've amassed a strong collection of domain names. It's time to make a profit, right? A business came up with a name for its firm that is a match for one of your names.

No, not always. The availability of a domain name isn't always important when coming up with a name, according to Altman and Shore. Some businesses don't care as much about domain names, even if they may do various checks for intellectual property along the process.

While it might be a mistake, this is the situation. Some businesses may choose a name that is comparable to their brand or uses a different extension than.com. Others don't need a separate website for the brand, particularly if the firm utilizes its primary brand name for its website and the brand in question is a sub-brand or a new product name.

Yet, most firms are concerned about the domain, particularly small ones with limited marketing budgets. The "exact match".com domain name is a nice-to-have for the business, even if nothing else.

Take Names
Many of the resources used by skilled names are now at your disposal. Put on your naming cap, brainstorm some great brand names for the future, and register your names with Namecheap right now.

The slogan/tagline should express your company in a line: 'Quality, perfumed candles produced to order', but might equally integrate an action for added pizzazz: 'Discover your new favorite wooly pullover'.

Brief Boxes

Decide on your top three selling points. Consider the concepts of service, quality, and delivery speed. These are items that are true, don't need much (or any) explanation, and try to address as many of the inquiries from the clients as they can. Strive to emphasize the questions "Are you trustworthy?" and "Do you have what I need?" in particular.

Generally Speaking

You may fully express your tone of voice in this brand-focused work. Although it may be entertaining, extravagant, and dramatic, try to make it succinct, direct, and pertinent as well. If you have too much to say, you may always elaborate on your company's history on your "About" page.

Your introduction should generally contain a brief (condensed) brand history, what motivates you to succeed, and why you're different. But, you should carefully write each sentence to be appealing to the reader. In this case, mentioning your personal characteristics is generally not the best use of space, but explaining how you make the items could be. The essential need is to instill enthusiasm and excitement around the actual work that your company produces.

Product Choice

Strive to highlight at least some of your "top sellers" on your homepage, not the least of which is so that visitors may see what you are offering right away. Even if they don't read your well crafted text, they can still interact with the graphics.

One thing to keep in mind is that if you sell products and don't include a section for product feeds on your homepage, you are guaranteeing that anyone who visits will need to click at least twice more to view product listings, and customers leave your site with each additional click they are required to make.

Add social sharing buttons on your sites and items so customers may share them on their social network. Link out to your own social media accounts as well to connect your whole digital presence.

Page Products

These are the pages that provide all the details about certain items. Set the environment for the ideal way to enjoy your goods on the product page. Keep in mind that if your items are handcrafted, you'll need even more descriptions as you won't have the luxury of assuming that your buyers are already acquainted with them.

Put an emphasis on features and advantages while discussing items. In contrast to benefits, which are what a product delivers to your consumer, features are what a product performs. So be sure to give clients enough room to really see how using your product would improve their lives.

You use this area to both create a narrative that is exclusive to your product and to subtly convey to your buyers how this product will improve their lives.

<u>Images</u>
While a picture really does say a thousand words, there are several things you can do to improve your ads. Use product photographs in particular to further the narrative nature of your description.

<u>What should your pictures depict?</u>

For the purpose of marketing your items, high-quality photos are valuable. Painting an idealized, story-driven depiction of how your product may be utilized can help your buyers genuinely see themselves using the thing.

If you can, consider showcasing your items being used by a customer or even in their natural environment. The more closely your photographs may resemble Disneyland in their theming, the better.

People will grasp size better if there is at least one photograph illustrating scale (the product in relation to other objects), which is particularly helpful if the item is homemade and there is no other clear reference to size.

Unless you clearly know they are copyright-free, all photographs, including those that aren't of your products, should always be your own. Yet distinctive, high-quality photographs, particularly those of items, may also aid in site SEO, particularly if you give them a catchy name and as much descriptive information as your CMS permits.

Various Site Essentials

Several components might help clients feel confident in your business in addition to the storefront. Several things that you may want to add are covered in depth on this blog. You should definitely at least include the following in order to keep it simple at first:

Contact page with the company address

To ensure authenticity, they are crucial. In order for you to be eligible for their service, any service you join up for, like Google Merchant will verify that you have an active email address (a contact box does not count).

It's simple enough to establish admin@yourbusiness.com if you, understandably, don't want to use a personal email there.

3. Spread the Word About Your Website

Promoting your e-commerce shop requires a lot of work and there aren't many one-size-fits-all strategies.

Hence, before you start spending money on advertising, try to place your site in the perspective of the larger Internet. Consider how you stack up against your rivals and what free tools you can use to increase awareness of your site.

Connect all of your social media accounts to your website and vice versa.
Connecting your digital footprint is a terrific concept if you want to gain from your current following. Promote your domain so

that search engines may begin to index it. You may even design special promotions and coupons exclusively for this group of people. Create social media accounts right away if you don't already have any; you'd be shocked at how many of your friends will be interested in your site before others. It may be really beneficial to get things started.

Sign up for Google Analytics.
Google Analytics allows you to follow every visitor to your website's path with a single line of code. It's free, and you may learn about each person's unique travels, how they discovered you, where they are, and much more. Even if this is more of a long-term objective, it's helpful to put everything up in the beginning so you have data from the get-go.

Register with Google Merchant.
Join them if you can't defeat them. Many, many individuals use Google Shopping to

discover things. You may offer your items the greatest chance of appearing in Google Shopping search results by registering for Google Merchant.

A simple plugin that encourages you to provide all the details that will assist your products perform the best on Google Merchant will help with this process if you're using WordPress and WooCommerce. While the most basic Google Merchant accounts are free, there are additional premium solutions available if you wish to subsequently enhance your listings.

Browse and Learn

These three ideas are only the proverbial top of a much larger iceberg. In the weeks and months ahead, as you work to make your eCommerce site successful, you should consider collaborating with bloggers and influencers, Google and Facebook marketing, and even affiliate programs.

After your website starts receiving some traffic, it's a good idea to check Google Analytics to evaluate how real behavior compares to your desired behavior. This will enable you to improve and modify the website in light of user feedback. An eCommerce site has the drawback of never being completed. To increase its sales potential, it is continuously improved and changed.

You'll discover the specifics that apply to your industry and scenario and create your own "handbook" of best practices. To help other people, feel free to share them as a comment at the conclusion of this blog.

Establish a Shop in an eCommerce Directory

For newbies, setting up business on a reputable eCommerce platform is a great choice. You merely need to join up, enter the company name, and list the items on the majority of marketplaces.

You may choose this option without worrying about the functionality and style of the website. Therefore it's appropriate for those who wish to dropship as a side business.

In order to reach a wider audience, dropshipping companies who already have their own website may decide to open an eCommerce shop on a marketplace.

The following are some key benefits of launching a dropshipping company on an online store:

high levels of traffic. Although eCommerce marketplaces cannot promise significant traffic, they already have a large user base. Customers are thus more likely to stop by your business while they browse the marketplace's website.

a long-standing clientele. These platforms have staff who are solely responsible for drawing clients and promoting the market. Many of the users of the site are already frequent, devoted buyers.

an effective infrastructure. Marketplaces for eCommerce already have the necessary infrastructure to handle transactions. Several allow you to sell globally and provide a variety of payment and delivery options.

Simple setup. Just register and adhere to the platform's guidelines. You won't have to bother about website design if you choose this option.

It's crucial to remember that an eCommerce marketplace might also have drawbacks.

Platform charges. The majority of eCommerce platforms deduct money from each transaction you make. Platform, handling, and transaction costs are part of these reductions. As a result, choosing this option will reduce your profit margin.

limited authority. Dropshippers have very little choice over branding, payment options, and delivery options since they must adhere to a rigid template provided by the marketplace.

Competition. Dropshippers must take into account other sellers on the marketplace who could offer the same goods. Customers may compare your items with those of other merchants in a marketplace with ease.

Lack of distinctiveness. It's more difficult for your dropshipping company to differentiate itself from the competition and build a solid brand when you stick to a predetermined template.

lack of faith. Some consumers may have doubts regarding the quality of the products since they see eCommerce marketplaces as venues for inexperienced firms.

Listed below are some of the most well-liked platforms for starting a dropshipping company, if you're interested in going this route:

1. Amazon

The most well-known eCommerce site is Amazon, which has more than 200 million Prime members globally. Follow Amazon's dropshipping guidelines if you decide to sell on this marketplace:

Packaging. On all packing slips, clearly identify your dropshipping company as the vendor.

completing orders. Taking orders and handling returns from customers is your responsibility.

Seller consent. Adhere with all conditions outlined in the seller agreement, as well as Amazon rules.

Depending on the sort of goods, there are different costs for selling it on Amazon, but they typically range from 10-15% of your sales. This charge has a significant impact on your pricing, particularly if you run a small firm with thin profit margins.

The Individual plan on Amazon costs $0.99 per item. As an alternative, there are no per-item fees with the Professional plan, which costs $39.99/month. Keep in mind that there can be extra expenses, such referral and delivery costs.

2. eBay

eBay is a well-known eCommerce site that is excellent for dropshipping businesses. This internet store practices consumer-to-consumer sales and has over 147 million active customers. Also, it offers an auction system where purchasers may place bids on products.

While being an excellent online store, eBay has limits on dropshipping. Order fulfillment must come only from wholesale suppliers for all dropshipping eCommerce companies.

Dropshippers cannot resale goods from another retail website or eCommerce platform on eBay. Moreover, all dropshippers are accountable for keeping in touch with clients and delivering goods securely and on schedule.

Note that if you violate eBay's drop shipping policy, it may delete or devalue your listings from its search results.

To sell on eBay, online shops must pay a fee; options begin at $4.95/month. eBay will impose insertion costs for each extra listing if the number of items you sell is more than the maximum specified in the plan.

3. AliExpress

Another well-liked marketplace for dropshipping eCommerce firms is AliExpress. The marketplace has more than 150 million active users despite being a platform that is less established than Amazon and eBay.

Dropshippers may quickly identify things to offer in their online shop using this platform. For assistance in starting a dropshipping company, the marketplace provides AliDropship.

Have in mind, nevertheless, that AliExpress is not renowned for its high-quality goods. Its primary selling point is cost, and the market is crowded.

Your competitive edge in an AliExpress dropshipping company is not your pricing or a line of distinctive items. The two areas to concentrate on to differentiate yourself from rivals are marketing and customer service.

Depending on the product category, AliExpress retains a fee of 5–8% on each sale. Keep in mind that the expenses of delivery, which vary based on the courier and location, are your responsibility.

How to Launch a Dropshipping Company and What to Avoid

Avoid the following when you launch a dropshipping company:

picking the incorrect niche. It's challenging to find clients in a vast or outmoded niche. By doing thorough market research, you may avoid picking the incorrect niche.

failing to optimize your store. In your online shop, customers should have the greatest possible experience. Make sure your shop prioritizes the demands of the consumers by optimizing each page.

excessive reliance on suppliers. Placing too much faith on your providers may be dangerous, therefore having backups is crucial. Write a contract with your suppliers so they are aware of your expectations in order to protect your company.

There is not enough branding. Branding is crucial in dropshipping to differentiate yourself from rivals. Customers may purchase the goods elsewhere, thus it's important to continuously communicate your brand.

inadequate client service. Get in touch with your consumers to make sure they are happy with your offerings.

Shipment problems. Before approving your customer's order, check with your supplier. This will lessen shipping-related problems.

You will increase your chances of launching a successful dropshipping company by staying away from these frequent blunders.

Chapter five

Conclusion

The dropshipping business strategy is a fantastic method to launch an online venture without having to handle inventory. As this post has shown, starting a dropshipping company is rather simple, making it suited for those with less business expertise and a smaller budget.

To summarize, choose a market niche for your firm and do market research to identify the kinds of goods you will offer. Finally, locate trustworthy dropshipping vendors to purchase your goods. Verify that they are reliable vendors that provide top-notch goods and services.

Don't forget to separate your money and register your company after you've begun building the shop. To guarantee long-term success, spend some effort marketing and promoting your company.

In addition, we have covered what to avoid and the advantages of starting a dropshipping company. We also discussed the advantages and disadvantages of the various platforms.

This post should have provided you with additional information about dropshipping and how to get started. Please leave a remark if you have any queries or advice. Good fortune!

Questions on How to Begin Dropshipping
Now that you are aware of how to launch a dropshipping company, let's address some often asked questions.

Is it Simple to Start Dropshipping?
One of the simplest ways to start an eCommerce shop is via dropshipping. Even

those with little resources and knowledge may build a low-risk dropshipping shop. Just establish the shop, take care of the legalities and money, choose a specialized supplier, and advertise the company.

Does Dropshipping Pay Off?
Undoubtedly, there are more advantages to starting a dropshipping company than disadvantages. There is lots of flexibility to expand your firm and swap out underperforming goods.

Can Dropshipping Be Profitable?
Dropshipping is a well-known successful business strategy. In actuality, dropshippers may profit by over 50% more than stock inventory owners. You will spend less than with other company models since you won't have to worry about warehousing charges or overstocking.

Is it Possible to Launch a Dropshipping Company for Free?

Yes, technically. You may start selling things right away with no inventory if you use the dropshipping business model. As a result, you don't buy the goods until you've gotten the customer's money. To avoid paying until you make a sale, you must choose an eCommerce platform.

www.ingramcontent.com/pod-product-compliance
Lightning Source LLC
Chambersburg PA
CBHW071047220526
45467CB00004B/1704